T0365332

Robert E. Gillis

BeerBobSpeaks

Print information available on the last page.

Rev. date: 06/28/2018

To order additional copies of this book, contact:
Xlibris
1-888-795-4274
www.Xlibris.com
Orders@Xlibris.com

ACKNOWLEDGEMENTS

Here is a warm Kansas City thank you to all my family, friends, and fans that helped make this book possible! Special thanks to Fanny Witherspoon, archivist at the Kansas City Star for her invaluable research assistance and great sense of humor. Thanks to Donna Stewart, editor at the Kansas City Call for donating several photos from their sports collection. To Geraldlyn "Geri'" Sanders at the Kansas City Art Institute, thanks so much for transcribing tapes and proofreading the first drafts. Thank you Dr. Zinna Bland at Central Missouri State University for helping to proof the final drafts. Thanks to Trendle Cady for her words of inspiration when it was needed most.

Thanks to Tina Ellsworth and Josh Malecki, graduate students at Central Missouri State University for shadowing me at the stadium for a "day in the life of Beer Bob" and for helping with some of the fan interviews. Thanks to Joshua Ostergaard, The Field Museum in Chicago, and Dr. Stephen Bird, Radford University, for your enthusiastic comments when I delivered my first talk on my book at the 16th Annual Cooperstown Symposium on Baseball and American Culture. Thanks to the excellent staff at Xlibris especially July Valasquez, Harold Corsame, Rob Gonzales, and Elaine Joy A. Nemenzo!

Thanks to Jeff Montgomery & Steve Palermo for your photos and support. You both have been a real inspiration. Thanks to "Preacher" who gave me my start in the business and Nate Dorsey, Clement Reed, Jack Malan, Mr. Kelow, as well as the late Mr. Holmes and Mr. Dillard who all helped me along the way. Thanks to Diana Lehman, former Community Relations Assistant for the Kansas City Royals, Steve Denny, Paula Gunlock, Jim Fisher, and Jim Cundiff, from Center Plate, formerly Volume Services, for helping me with the business of baseball.

Thanks so much to all of the wonderful fans who generously shared their memories, stories, and photos with me especially Lou Steel, Glenn, Mary, Chuck Queen, Jimi Frantze, Steve & Dianne Fortner, Roger Potter, Jenny Burkhead, Tripp & Dia Hogue, Nick Moos & Judy Jones. Please forgive me if I left anyone out. This book's for you!

The book is also dedicated to my Uncle Earnest Houston (1917-2003)

who started his baseball career in 1947 with the Memphis Red Sox.

Robert "Beer Bob" Gillis

CONTENTS

Since the summer of 1996, I have thought about writing a book that tells about my experiences as a Beer vendor at the old Royals-now Kauffman Stadium. I was very pleased when we named the Stadium after Ewing Kauffman. Without "Mr. K" baseball would never have stayed in Kansas City. While there have been a lot of books written on the players, coaches and even ball club owners, very little has been written about our national pastime from the perspective of the everyday people-THE FANS -who live the game daily. So this is my contribution to the subject.

My first day with the Kansas City Royals Baseball Team began on April 10, 1978; I had a blue uniform on and was ready to work. I had my beer opener, my ID, and my hat, I was ready to walk many miles throughout the stands to meet and greet the fans. I had Pabst Blue Ribbon to sell on opening day.

There was a crowd of over 38,000 looking for a beer, and I was ready to sell. It was a time that was a real awakening for me - my first day. I had seen the Baltimore Orioles many times at the stadium as a young man growing up. We looked for a win out of these guys. I knew the Royals had an opportunity to have a World Series team that year. We had played the last two years like a championship team.

There were fans all over the Midwest, from as far away as Texas and Oklahoma to Nebraska to Kansas to Iowa and even Colorado. The parking lot was filled with license plates from all over. I've seen license plates from Canada, and license plates from Connecticut. I see license plates from all over when we walk back to our cars to go home after a game. There are Royal fans all over this United States. "You gotta love these guys."

These are just some of my oldest customers, like Nick and Judy, Tripp and Di.

I can remember the fans at Royals Stadium with the series; they were looking for Beer Bob for another beer or two. We would stop and sell three or four, and we would chat a little here and there. We would talk about how we believed the Royals would make it through the series fast. We were all good, and the game was so nice, I just knew these guys had something magical inside. We looked and we talked and pondered on the game, we knew this team was just coming back game after game. They would never roll over and they would never quit, the fans would say "Hey, don't give up." We haven't yet!

One thing about Beer Bob over the years, I have worked both sides of the Stadium, and I can say I have done great on both sides of both stadiums, working with the fans and selling beer to them and talking with fans over the years. Fans I consider friends. I have worked left field GA, right field GA, left field, third base line, left field, out in the outfield, right field, behind first base line and home plate, and even in the upper deck. I have worked all over our great stadium and really have enjoyed the time so I hope you will enjoy this book of memories.

First, let me tell you a little about myself and how I got started. Well, I am not just a baseball fan. I love sports-all kinds of sports!!! I was born in 1953 and raised in Kansas City on the Westside of town. This working class area was an ethnically diverse community of white, black and Hispanic Americans. So I grew up learning about all kinds of people during America's civil rights years in the 1950s and 1960s, a time for dramatic change.

After my dad Sam died when I was just a young kid. My mom, Virginia raised my brothers, my baby sister and me. You can see her with me, my brothers Lonnie and Michael with my sister Sharon. My older brother Richard and my late brothers Samuel and Jesse are not in the picture. In the early 1960s, we were able to move into the new Pennway Plaza development on the Westside because my Dad was a World War II veteran. My mom got priority status. She said, "We were one of the first black families to move into the development."

My mother was a strict disciplinarian. You know "spare the rod and spoil the child." She was also the "neighborhood mom" and it didn't matter what race you were. She was a mom to my friend here Steve Fortner owner of Steve's Floral Shop located downtown on Baltimore. Steve has on the striped sweater. He is pictured here with his brothers and sister Danny, Debbie, and Bennett. His brother Bill is not in the picture. Steve and I often talk about how we made it out of the Pennway Plaza Projects on the Westside.

My mom made sure that me and my brothers stayed out of trouble by having us play baseball, basketball, football and even boxing. I come from a family of athletes. My uncle, the late Earnest Houston played in the Negro Leagues for the Memphis Red Sox. I had cousins who boxed, ran track, played basketball and football. All of my brothers were athletes so it was no surprise that I lettered in every sport at West High School. My brothers and I are actually Golden Glove Champions. We trained under the legendary Arrington "Bubbles" Klice, and Mr. Nix, but that's a story for another book. I did well in school and loved all sports, but my sister reminded me that I treasured my baseball cards most. She said "I would go in my room and close the door and spread them out all over the floor."

After the 1968 race riots, Ewing Kauffman helped fund an inner city youth program. I think Robert Rhoades the general manager of Armco Steel helped too. Felix Stickney was the director of the program at the Paseo-Linwood YMCA Branch. So, it was fun to be a part of the Y-Royals and go to the Municipal Stadium and watch the Royals play. I really appreciate "Mr. K" bringing major league baseball back to Kansas City. And over the years, it was always nice to see Ewing & Muriel Kauffman out at the stadium. In 1973, the Royals stadium opened just east of downtown. I remember seeing some of the old players like Al Fitzmorris, Cookie Rojas, Lou Piniella, and of course my all-time favorite first basemen, John Mayberry pictured here.

Anyway, I graduated from West High School in 1971. I thought about attending Langston University in Oklahoma where my mom's family is from, but I got a baseball scholarship to Lincoln University in Jefferson City. I studied pre-law and environmental studies. Like most athletes, I knew I was headed to the major leagues. However, in my junior year I returned home to help my Mom out financially and to play a father role for my younger siblings. At home, I am called "Big Bad Bob" because I am a leader and take-charge kind of guy. Obviously, leaving college changed the direction of my future, but I have no regrets.

Instead of playing professional baseball, I coached kids in my spare time for over three decades in Sac 20: Ghetto to Goldmine program, the Ernie Mel League, the Boys & Girls Club RBI League, the Ambassadors 4 Christ league, at the Lykins Community Center, and the Troost-Midtown Community Center.

I also got a job for the City of Kansas City. I retired in 2003 after 30 years as a Code Enforcement Officer. For most of my career I worked in the Neighborhood and Community Service Division including the Community Action Network (CAN), the Local Law Enforcement Block Grant Program, and Operation Clean Sweep. I have worked all over the city including the inner city and Historic Old Northeast. My last assignment was in the Dangerous Buildings Demolition and Preservation on Prospect Avenue. After working an eight-hour day though, I was ready to head to my second job at the stadium.

Professionally, I have always held leadership positions like helping to found the Missouri Association of Code Enforcement (MACE), or serving at the national level of the American Association of Code Enforcement. I was always active in the union, too and worked just as long as a union steward, arbitrator and negotiator. My pre-law training really paid off. In 2002, I was elected President of the American Federation of State, County, and Municipal Employee (AFSCME) Local 500, the largest union in Kansas City representing almost 2000 employees.

And then a few years ago, I decided I wanted to spend my retirement years with the love of my life. This is Beer Bob down on bended knee asking "my sweetie, Dee" to marry me in front of 26,009 fans at the Texas Rangers game on September 9, 2000. That night a lot of fans asked me for autographs. And best of all Delia, said yes!!!! That was a relief because it had not been very long since I had seen a fan ask his best girl and she said "no"- wow what an embarrassment in front of thousands of people. Another fan teased me about the diamonds in the engagement ring, he said, "Bob that must of cost you all of your beer money." Yeah, maybe so, but it was worth it!

Kauffman Stadium

Special Messages

Beer Bob -
Happy
Father's Day!

Love,
Dee

The stadium is the center of our family life, too. Birthdays, Anniversaries, Mothers Day, Memorial Day, Fathers Day, Fourth of July, Labor Day, everyday is a Royals day for my wife and our kids Colin, Robert Jr., and Jasmine.

12

Now I am a vendor enjoying my path, enjoying the fans so graciously. From April until October, I arrive at Kaufman Stadium for every Royals home game almost an hour before game time so I can go to the "bullpen," which is located under the lower level seats, and get stocked for the game with Bud Light. I will make several trips back to get more beer and ice for my tray. Over the years, I have carried different brands in the bottle and in the can.

My fans are great. I knew this from the start that April 10th in 1978. What captured my eyes, what captured my thoughts was selling beer and fans saying, "Hey beer man, got a beer? We need a beer here." "Hey Sir, can I have a beer please?" and I said, "Yes Sir, I got one coming right up for you." We had bottled beer and cups galore. If you needed a beer, I was there to serve and more. "Guess what, sir; the beer is only, .80. Here's a beer for you. Thank you!"

In 1978, when I was looking to make some extra money, "Preacher" a friend and a beer man, got me a job out at old Royals Stadium and I been there ever since on the front lines watching every play serving my loyal fans. And Nate Dorsey helped me along the way. I thought I would also mention my friend Arch. He is a beer man. We have had a little competition with each other over the years, but we are best friends. Arch is my friend and true buddy, just a great guy. Fans don't forget about him. He is a personal friend, a close friend, like a brother. Arch and I are the top sellers in the stadium. This is my buddy Arch. He missed my good customers Glenn and his wife, because they are waiting on me, Beer Bob.

And there are lots of fans that will only buy their beer from me like Tom who moved from Atlanta to Kansas City in 1994. Hey, the fans consider me their personal vendor. They appreciate my friendly face and knowledge about the game. One of my customers, Joyanne says, "I am a funny guy." My biggest night was 25 cases during a Yankee doubleheader. Beer men like me have helped to make "millions of dollars" for the franchise.

I remember my first encounter with some long time fans, as I said about 1978. There were fans to remember like Trip. There are fans of ours now that are still avid Royals fans. Trip was coming to the games even prior to my working there and selling beer. He had Mary, Mickey, Nick and Judy with him. They sat in general admission (GA) and they had a great season. Now I serve them in section 120L. .

In 1978, I was named Beer Bob. There was a fan that went back a lot of years, and we called him "Santa Claus." I am sure you all remember him. He had a crew of fans that sat with him. One of his friends was a cousin of Royals player Al Cowens. There was another young man that sat with him; and hey, you talk about guys who drank some beer. Santa Claus never drank, but his crew did. That is how my name came about; the legend of Beer Bob was born and began. "Beer Bob" Santa Claus called me. I would come up and down the stairs working with Nate Dorsey, Jack Malan, Clement Reed, and Mr. Holmes, some of the guys who taught me and started me in this career. One thrill by the minute, we cherished that name Beer Bob every minute. Now all along the first base row and all over the stadium, my fans scream my name BEER BOB!

Can't you see my good friend enjoying a nice cold Bud Light? After all, what is baseball without the beer? Beer Bob knows! Not only the fellas, but ladies too! Take a look at these four fans. Hey, it's ladies' night out and their cups our filled to the brim courtesy of their favorite BEER MAN-They scream we love you BEER BOB!

Fouls balls can be a real hazard for beer men. I have been hit only twice by a ball. Actually, one fell into my cooler and another recently hit me in the shoulder. I turned around and did the Arnold Schwarzenegger "Flex" to show my fans I was okay. They just smiled and cheered when they knew I was fine and said, "Keep the beer flowing."

Now as I was saying the Beer Man has serious clout in the stadium. Just look at these fellas waiting on me. I am the number one Beer Man for many reasons. These guys are waiting on me-BEER BOB for their Beer--no one pours it quite the way BEER BOB does! Can I serve you a nice ice cold Bud Light? How about it? Beer Bob is here, how about an ice-cold beer? It's Bud Light. Beer Bob's back. I am here to serve you some beer. How about a Bud Light? It's ice cold. Come on and get it. May I help you? Would you like to have a cold beer?

Now some people might think that being a Beer Man is a lowly job-Well I beg to differ! We are at the heart and soul of the game. We are out there game after game, more than 80 games every year. And if you take a look at the photo, my good friend Roger Potter started out as a BEER MAN and worked his way through law school! He is a really great attorney. And here is my good friend Jimi Frantze ready to throw the first pitch of the game. His Italian restaurant Frondizi's on the Plaza is my favorite place to take my wife on special occasions.

All of my friends that come to Kauffman Stadium enjoy the atmosphere and all of its amenities. Kauffman Stadium is one of the most beautiful stadiums in the country with fountains and a huge Sony JumboTron. The grass—the aroma from the fields makes us a dream team with natural grass. Thanks to the ground crew. Like Dan Quisenberry said, "Natural grass is a wonderful thing for little bugs and sinkerball pitchers." It is just wonderful to have your friends come out and enjoy Kansas City baseball and its pleasures. Beer Bob says, "Fans come out, one and all. Come out to this beautiful stadium that we have—to Kauffman Stadium in the Truman Complex."

In 1979, there was a day I will always remember, we called it "Halter Top Day" and you can bet you I will remember. We had almost 40,000 fans watching the show. I believe Splittorff was on the mound to pitch that day. What a show. Fans came from all around and women came from all over town to get their halter-tops that said "Royals" across the top. It was amazing to me, I was selling a lot of beer, but I can tell you this, those halter tops mysteriously appeared. The ladies had them on throughout the game, so guess where they had to change to put them on. So if you missed that day, as a day to remember, Beer Bob will never forget that magical experience of Halter Top Day in Royals history in 1979. That was May 20th of 1979. It was Halter Top Day, 40,000 fans turned the turnstiles to cheer the Royals on to another victory. I believe the score was 5-1, but guess what, the most exciting time was Halter Top Day.

It was a magical time out at Royals Stadium. When the game started, the halter-tops were passed out through the gate and through the turnstile, but before the game started, there were halter-tops on and the game was going on and it was an exciting time. It was a magical time in Royal history and I will never forget my time at Royal Stadium on my first Halter Top Day. Thanks you Royal fans, thank you so much. I enjoyed seeing those halter tops so much. I believe I sold thirteen cases that glorious day, and there was plenty of beer flowing throughout the day.

In 1985 in the Toronto series, I was selling beer on the left field side of third base line and I was down around about the dugouts on the left field side and there was a fan that stole one of my beers. We were selling bottle beer, it was a Bud Light and the fan took the beer, left it open, poured it out in the cup that he had and then had the nerve to put the empty bottle back in my case. But several wonderful Royals fans saw him and knew the guy had been drinking. I would not have served the guy because it looked like the guy had too much to drink. I asked the guy, "What are you doing. If you really need that beer you can have the beer."

The guy got smart and lied and said he didn't take the beer, but all the fans were pointing at him. Three or four fans pointed this guy out to the police. I went all the way up there to give the police a report …and they pointed this guy out. He just refused to talk so they took him out. What was really bad about the whole situation was that the guy had to go to court. I had to take off work early so I could attend the hearing when the guy went before the judge. The judge asked him, "The Royals are trying to go to the World Series and this man is out there working and making a living and you are stealing a beer-one beer?" Let me tell you something son, it will cost you $500." The guy said he did not have $500 so the judge told the bailiff to lock him up. Until he gets the money, he will be locked up.

That was kind of interesting to me, stealing one beer from the beer man that's working hard trying to serve beer to the Royals fans, other customers, and other fans. I guess that guy learned a valuable lesson. He apologized in court; he said that he was kind of "reckless."

Take me out to the ballgame. I wanna have a hot dog, I wanna have some beer, I wanna have some peanuts and I wanna cheer. I am here to say, go Royals go. I am here to say, win Royals win. I am here to say strike three ump, make sure the Royals' pitch is in. I am here to say we love our team so dear, I am here to say, we cannot do without our Beer.

I remember back in 1995, the Famous Chicken came out to the Stadium and even on bad nights when the Royals plummeted— and they got plummeted that day—I think we scored one run and Oakland A's scored 11, but the Famous Chicken is always great and fantastic, and fans still enjoyed themselves even though we got blowed out that day.

21

It is always a pleasure to see the Chicken. That Chicken, he is a funny, funny guy. Interacting with the fans. I can remember he was here in 1999, I was selling beer down by the dugout and he was up on the dugout, he was just funny. Doing tricks and some fantastic things. It just seems like the fans do come out to see the Chicken. They come out to enjoy themselves with their children and their parents and families to see this guy perform and enjoy themselves at a day or a night game. He has done a great job and I really enjoy that along with the fans. I try to get a laugh or two before I go back to selling. Fans like Caroline, Jose, and Jenny were even on ESPN looking for the Chicken.

It was really great when the Royals had Bat Day at the Stadium. I wish they would bring back those days. The children loved getting those bats. They paid a high price for those bats, but the children loved them. I remember when I used to get bats at the baseball games. They were Royal blue bats that are really fantastic. I just wish that is something they could bring back sometimes, every three years or so, bring it back for the kids and the kids at heart. There are sponsors out there that could do that. The Royals, I am sure, can get that done for little fans like Keri, Brian, and Dustin.

Fireworks, man that is great; every Friday night. I just wish the Royals could do it every Friday and Saturday night. Do it for the fans those two nights, after the games. It is just great. The beer men wait until after the games are over and watch the fireworks. That is just fantastic! The Royals, keep doing that and lets add another day. Come on Royals. We love you here in Kansas City and just having fireworks over the entire weekend that would be just great.

Also Kansas City Royals fans, go visit the Negro Leagues Baseball Museum in the historic 18th & Vine district where the legendary Buck O'Neal lives. Buck comes out to Royals Stadium, charting pitchers, charting players. Every summer, we celebrate the Negro Leagues at the stadium to honor those great players like Jackie Robinson, Satchel Paige, Josh Gibson, Earnest Houston, Frank Duncan, and Buck O'Neil. Royals, it is really a great idea giving the fans a hat from the old Kansas City Monarchs. Buck is a patriarch of Kansas City baseball; this guy is tremendous, a real goodwill ambassador for the city. Beer Bob says, "Please, go out and support that museum at 1616 East 18th Street.

BEER BOB'S BEST

Besides all of the wonderful fans, I like to see my favorite players, too. Beer Bob's All Time All Star Royals line-up would be John Mayberry on first base, Frank White on second base, U.L. Washington and Freddie Patek as shortstop, George Brett on Third Base, Willie Wilson in Left Field, Amos Otis in Center Field, Al Cowens in Right Field, Hal McRae is my Designated Hitter, Darrell Porter is my catcher, and six pitchers round out my team, Dennis Leonard, Bret Saberhagen, Paul Splittorff, Steve Busby, Dan Quisenberry and Jeff Montgomery.

Jeff Montgomery stayed with Kansas City and had a great slider. He is a real stand-up guy and it was so exciting to see him and his family when he was inducted into the Royals Hall of Fame in 2003. And he is still dedicated to baseball behind the scenes in Kansas City with Royals baseball radio 810am. When I am headed home after the game, I always tune in to hear the final results from Denny Matthews or Ryan Lefebvre. Jeff Montgomery and fans Jimi Frantze, Rich Duvall, and Chuck Queen have been long time supporters of my little league teams. Thanks guys!

Our "royal son," George Brett is a favorite. This is a shot of George Brett (5) rounding the base at the championship game.

Next to George Brett, one of my favorite players is Frank White, homegrown from Kansas City just like me. It has been great seeing him on the coaching staff, too. As you can see in this shot, Frank White had a lot of showmanship on the field.

Amos Otis known as AO, another favorite player. He could hit and he just glided across the grounds when he caught a ball in centerfield. If the ball was over the fence, he would snatch it back. Yeah, but sad times are a part of the game too and here AO is with his teammates contemplating how are we gonna beat those damn Yankees!

Now take a look at my designated hitter, Hal "MAC" McRae, getting ready to unload a homerun straight into the beautiful fountain. McRae is on his way to bat and Sam Lacey an old KC KINGS basketball player is hanging around the dugout. Hustlin' HAL headed to third-saaaafe!

You know McRae played for the Royals from 1973 until 1987. He came back in 1991 to manage the team until 1994. It was pretty special to have McRae around! The icing on the cake was that he managed his son Brian who played for the Royals from 1990 to 1994. Brian started out as a second baseman, but what an outfielder.

Like I said, AO is one of my favorite Royals of all time, besides George Brett, Frank White and Jeff Montgomery. When he got under a ball, it looked like he was there so fast and so quick. Just floating to get to the ball. Anything in the stadium he caught. If it was near him, he had it. His bat was like a ringing power of wood.

I remember AO was sick over at St. Luke's Hospital. This guy passed a kidney stone, wow what a thought. You know how painful those things can be whenever you are sick and really out. However, he came back with his grace and glory, AO bombed a three-run homer and the Royals made it two in a row over the dreaded Baltimore Orioles. Dennis Leonard was the winning pitcher in a crowd of 17,440 fans. What an exciting time I thought and what an exciting time it was. Beer Bob was selling again.

Besides Leonard and Montgomery, one of my favorite pitchers of all time was Steve Busby. I watched him as a teenager and beer man. I remember one game he was really hurting around the shoulder and all, and guess what, they brought up a rookie named Rich Gale. No one believed Gale had the stamina to stay and become a big leaguer and win games for the Kansas City Royals like Steve had done previously. Maybe the magic was there; maybe the magic had always been there for that pitcher who moved into that slot because Rich Gale was a great pitcher, even though he was not around a lot. But for that year in 1978 this amazing young rookie, 6'7" in height brought that ball down and it was a strike. This guy pitched hard, and he pitched strong and that was amazing.

I can also say the "Mad Hungarian" was a pitcher with great aspirations. This guy would get so hyped, the mound would shake and the fans would quiver when old Al Hrabosky would throw his hot subliminous flame pitch across the plate. There were some disappointing players like Andy Hassler, Jim Colborn, and Steve Mingori. Even though these players helped us get to the pennant, I thought they could have done more to help us finish. Highlight pitchers, you know, Leonard, Paul Splittorff, Gura, Gale, and Hrabosky were Beer Bob's favorite pitchers of the year.

Besides the players, you gotta love the umpires. Of course at the top of my list is Steve Palermo. Yeah, he could not only make a close call, he could blow one mean bubble on that gum. I was actually at home when a news flash came over the TV that Palermo had been shot in Arlington, Texas, while trying to help two waitresses who were being robbed. What a stand up guy! What a real life hero! Not just a great UMP, but also a friend.

Now this old veteran UMP George Malloy, players and fans loved how he kept the game moving. This is my friend Trip getting his autograph. Since 1975, Trip has been a die hard Royals Fan and he likes beer so much that he works for Boulevard Brewery on Southwest Boulevard!

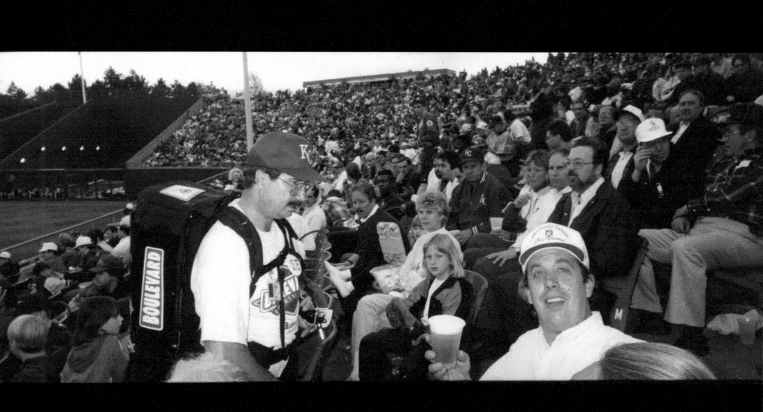

1985 World Series, These guys slammed us at home. The fat lady hadn't sung yet and we beat the St. Louis Cardinals 4 games to 3.

Beer Bob says it's all about what's happening. If you believe in a team, you can be happy. You know, we might have lost in 1984 and in 1980, but in 1985, we stepped up to give our own Kansas City chapter. It was a "Show Me" I-70 series I will never forget. You have St. Louis on one end and Kansas City on the other. It is a rivalry you see, I-70 thriller coming to the Show-Me State. The Show-Me State was great; the games were great with one of the greatest series you ever saw.

But to really appreciate that sweet sweet victory, you have to stop and think back to 1980 when we were the American Leagues Champions and came so close to winning a World Series Championship. You have to think about all of the great talent on our team even in 1978 and some exciting matches throughout the '80s especially 1984.

1978, Larry Gura was so good he pitched 16 victories. What a thrill, what a thrill! That was Rich Gale, the young rookie, coming up pitching strong, this guy almost had 15 victories, and he had 14 you know. And the Mad Hungarian came out strong. He was a wild man, but he was really strong. You had Marty Pattin, The Duck. You had Steve Busby who went down the earlier part of the year. But like I said, who came up to save us, Rich Gale, 6'7 extraordinare.

You could hear it sting when he hit the ball it was like a ringing sensations and the ball would fly off his bat. Singles, doubles, triples, it did not matter. When you thought the ball was so high up it floated right out and it was long gone out of the park. Otis was one of my favorite players. He had speed. He had power. He was a 5-tool player! I could not ever imagine that the Royals would have. But we did. And AO was a player to treasure. This guy won many a game, I can remember and recall.

Frank White was steady throughout his career. His bat was fantastic and his pivots were always a thrill. We had U.L. Washington at shortstop. Double-play combination, that's what we called them. They were really moving that ball across the infield again and again. I loved to see him stroke and clutch hit when we needed to have a win.

George Brett floated throughout the 1980 season trying to stabilize that .400 average.

We moved into the playoffs against the Yankees you know. What a dreaded team we wanted to beat so. These guys were brash. These guys were bullish. We thought they had Kansas City's number again and again and again. We tricked them this time with our expertise. It was October the 8th, the first playoff opener game. That happened on a Wednesday we were ready to see. Jim Frey gave the ball to Larry Gura to start the game to pitch against those dreaded Yankees and Rod Guidry again. Gura had a winning record of 18 and 10 and he loved to beat those Yankees again and again. We started off strong. We jumped right on Guidry again. Otis doubled; Aikens brought him home again.

We were as happy as can be when Willie Wilson doubled with Porter and White in the eighth and brought that game home and a victory for us. Hey, hey, hey Yankees, you are one down right now. Look whose coming next; it is Leonard's turn now. Leonard pitched so well and he pitched so well. You know what, we won against those Yankees at Royals Stadium again. The score was 3-2, a victory for Leonard again. Hey man think about it two games to zero; the Royals are heading to New York to see if we can close the deal.

I remember sitting at home watching the game on TV, saying we are going to win the game tonight you wait and see. Our guys were ready to play. They were ready to hit. You know what happened? We won again. I can recall that Otis had a good series. This guy batted, he had six hits and 11 bats in the series. But what I can remember and recall is Brett's tremendous home run off of Goose Gossage into the upper deck of Yankee Stadium. YEEEAH! Hey, hey, hey, we are headed to the Series now. Come on home, so we can play ball again.

The first World Series in 1980, what an experience! The Royals came to town down 0 to 2 in a series record with the Phillies. Well we started off and game three, guess what, we beat those Phillies 4-3 and it seemed Otis was as hot as can be, he and Willie Aikens were the stars you see Otis had three homers in the series and his average was about .478 throughout the series. He was 11 for 23, what an exciting thing to be. Otis and Aikens had about 22 total bases. Aikens was really a star, too. Willie "Mays" Aikens was the first player to have multi-homer games, in World Series history. Wow! They even put his bat in the Baseball Hall of Fame. McRae had a good series also. Clint Hurdle finished up strong, too. Brett was over .375. If we had a healthy Brett we could have won the series I am sure. The guys did well and we moved on strong. We may have lost the series, but we were still strong.

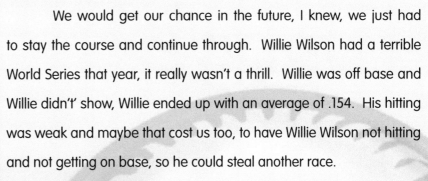

We would get our chance in the future, I knew, we just had to stay the course and continue through. Willie Wilson had a terrible World Series that year, it really wasn't a thrill. Willie was off base and Willie didn't' show, Willie ended up with an average of .154. His hitting was weak and maybe that cost us too, to have Willie Wilson not hitting and not getting on base, so he could steal another race.

So ironically we lost, hurting in heart. I knew it another time would come up and we would get our chance to take them all out. 42,000 fans each game came through. Beer Bob was selling beer to all of you. I want to thank you again for my series experience. I want to thank my fans that came through the turnstiles again and again. We may have not closed the deal and closed the show, but we knew someday we would get our chance.

In '84 we had some young gloves to arrive. Bret Saberhagen, Mark Gubicza, Bud Black and Dan Quisenberry were already there. Gura was a mainstay and Splittorff was there. Charlie Leibrandt was still on the mound but think and think hard, we had some young gloves that were ready to take it on. It was a dark day for me in 1984. Brett was hurt and also AO, Amos Otis, was not on the Royals team for 1984. However, the young and upstart Willie Wilson started his climb to glory. I latched onto him as one of my favorite players in Royals history. White was still there and there were some upstarts on the way. Steve "Bye-Bye" Balboni. George was hurt part of the season. That hurt us down the stretch. Sheridan was in right; Brett came in and was batting and knocking balls all around. Hal McRae was still the DH now and then and hitting and stinging the ball once again.

Again, I will begin in 1985, we thought about what and how we could survive. We had Danny Jackson, we had Brett, Saberhagen, we had Splittorff, and we had Mark Gubicza. The young gloves were ready and the veterans were prepared, we just knew we had a season that would last and last. "Quiz" was the man. He would strike you out with that sinker and the next thing you know, you were out of sight.

We had a new crop of Royals we could latch onto to feel happy and believe we had a great season coming. Willie was there; he was striking up a band. We made it to first place; we won again. We know we waited until the playoffs and we looked down the stretch with the Detroit Tigers, the Detroit Tigers I could not stand. All I could think about is that we could sweep these guys, but we got swept 3 and out. Willie Wilson batted over .300 that year and like I said, we thought we had another World Series appearance coming soon.

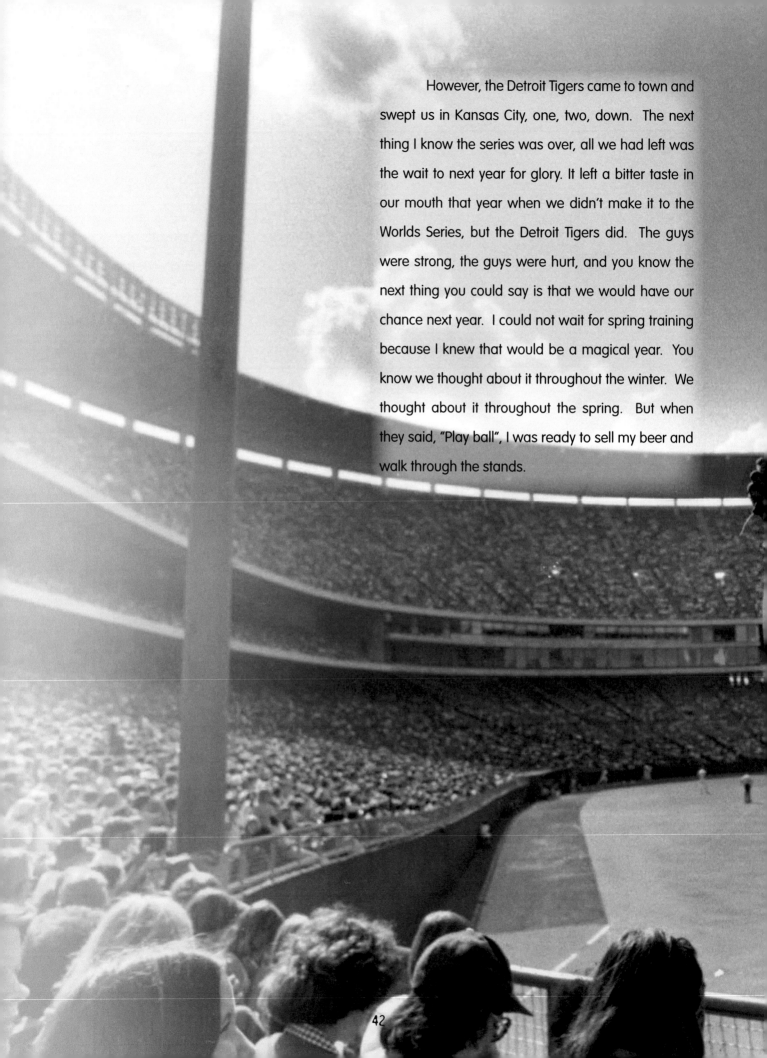

However, the Detroit Tigers came to town and swept us in Kansas City, one, two, down. The next thing I know the series was over, all we had left was the wait to next year for glory. It left a bitter taste in our mouth that year when we didn't make it to the Worlds Series, but the Detroit Tigers did. The guys were strong, the guys were hurt, and you know the next thing you could say is that we would have our chance next year. I could not wait for spring training because I knew that would be a magical year. You know we thought about it throughout the winter. We thought about it throughout the spring. But when they said, "Play ball", I was ready to sell my beer and walk through the stands.

Look at the fans! We knew our time had come in 1985. And this is none other than a cousin of former Royals player Al Cowens waving a victory flag!

Here we go!

You know the season did not look very promising from the start.

The Royals went into the second half of the season with a 44-42 record. But Bye-Bye Balboni went on a hot streak during the second half-knocking the cover off the ball. He also had a season record with 36 homers for a right-hander. I can recall a game in April that season when the Boston Red Sox came to Royals Stadium. Balboni hit a homer off of Roger Clemens, "the rocket." The Royals won 2-0 and stopped their four game losing streak. Darryl Motley, Pat Sheridan, and Lynn Jones worked hard in the outfield. Buddy Biancalana was a strong shortstop and Dane Iorg was the pinch hitter.

Two trades also made a real difference on the team. We acquired Jim Sunberg from the Milwaukee Brewers and he was one of the best defensive catchers in the game. John Schuerholz and Dick Howser worked on the line-up and we acquired Lonnie Smith to tighten up our number 2-hitter spot. We also

released Larry Gura. I was disappointed about that move. Howser also changed the line-up and rotated Hal McRae and Jorge Orta. Quisenberry was the showstopper and game saver; he had some relief help from the bullpen from Mike Jones, Joe Beckworth and Steve Farr.

The Royals won the regular season by one game over the California Angels with a 91-71 record. We were headed to the playoffs against the Toronto Blue Jays. We went to Toronto and in the last two games we swept those guys! We were on our way to the World Series in 1985. Again we came home at World's Series time, another World Series. This would be our time! Beer Bob was so happy! So were all the fans!

We lost that first game at home, 3-1, don't you know. We turned around and lost again at home to the Cardinals the score was 4-2, so much sorrow. Then we caught trains and we caught busses, we caught planes to St. Louis to see the game. Guess what, Kansas City won 6-1 in St. Louis for our first victory in the series. We lost again the next night and in Game 4, they shut us out 3-0. Oh my Lord, what a hurting feeling! We were down 3-1 and we knew we were down, but not out of the series yet. Guess what, a curve. The next night in St. Louis, Game 5 was awesome, 6-1. We left them in the dust! They had to take the champagne home because it was their loss that night!

We go home again and Beer Bob was selling beer. I sold so much beer, Beer Bob was as happy as can be. The crowd was magic, electricity flowed throughout the stadium, rafters and seats and fans. We knew we had a chance, but we were down 1-0. In the bottom of the ninth we came through with two runs you know. Dane Iorg was the man. He hit a single and brought in the 2 runs. It was awesome! We ended with a score of 2-1. The Royals won one more game. We were still in it to win it!

Sunday, October 27th, 1985 oh what a big night! We were filled with anticipation. Dick Howser had done it. We beat the Cardinals 11-0. What a shutout in the "I-70 series!" The game was tense and tight. The Cardinals' Whitey Herzog and Joaquin Andujar were ejected! Darryl Motley hit a tremendous home run! Saberhagen pitched a great game, a 5- hitter. The Cardinals used up 5 pitchers and still they could not stop us. We were so happy to go home a winner. We sent the Cardinals packing to St. Louis as we uncorked our champagne bottles in celebration of the Kansas City Royals' first World Series Championship!

In 1985, the year that Beer Bob will never forget, first place, 91 wins, 71 losses and a .562 winning percentage. The team broke a lot of records including: most intentional walks (31) by George Brett and Dan Quisenberry with the most games played (84) and the most games finished (77). The Royals ended the season with the fewest runners left on the base (1057) and the fewest singles (920). Brett and Howser were All-stars. Saberhagen was named series MVP and he won the Cy Young Award! Our team was set on coming back and winning this series, winning everything! It started out as a tough year, but look at the numbers again, 2,162, 717 fans came through the turnstiles. Beer Bob will never ever forget it! Royals' fans will never forget it and we loved our team for this victory. We had a big rally with the Royals at Liberty Memorial at the end of the World Series. It was fantastic! I will never forget thousands and thousands of fans out there. Beer Bob really enjoyed it!

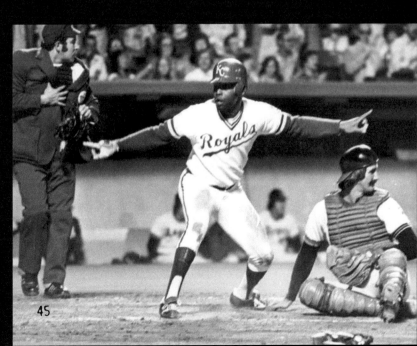

I remember the fans in '85, Tripp, Nick and other fans throughout the stadium that knew Beer Bob liked to sell beer. These fans were happy, these fans were glad. Think about it for a minute, all the glorious times we had. We sold a lot of beer throughout the year. We had a lot of friends pass through the Royals turnstile gates to see the games that were so clear. It may have rained, it may have sleeted, it may have been cold or it may have been so hot until it would make you want to take your shirt right off. But guess what, we had fun, we enjoyed our time. I think about those times and want them to come back some day again.

In 1986, I thought we were going to have another huge year. However, it did not materialize that way. We wound up coming in third place, but those things happen. We still had much the same team, but added a few players. Buddy Biancalana was still there and Darryl Motley and Lynn Jones and guess what, Bo Ja ckson made his appearance in Kansas City. He only played a short time, but we wound up coming in third place in 1986, so that was an enjoyable time to see Bo and just think about was coming next. George had a so, so year, he batted a .290 in 1986 and again in 1987. We still had some of our stable guys in the lineup, and 1987 was a full year for Bo Jackson.

One of the most disappointing years in Royals history for me was 1990 because we had so much potential and didn't fulfill the promise to Ewing Kauffman to win the pennant in the World Series again. We spent so much money for two players. One player came from the A's and the other player came from the San Diego Padres. Can you name those two players? The player from the San Diego Padres was Mark Davis and the player from the Oakland A's was Storm Davis—the Davis Boys.

A bad year: 1994 was another strike year. I can understand to some degree, but still it was devastating for the beer man to lose out on those games. It hurt then. I know baseball players did not always make a lot of money and I can understand their need to earn more and control the value of their talent, but isn't there a better way to solve these differences. Bidding wars between owners for star players creates some of the salary problems. Since this is entertainment, players should earn as much as they can.

The Royals had a third place finish, 64 wins and 51 losses. They could have won the championship that year, .557 winning percentage, four games back and still came out even with the strike year. We had 1,400,490 fans come through the turnstiles with a strike still going on; the beer men were out there mingling with so many fans. When I started with the Royals, which is when the 2 million fans really started coming out to the Stadium and before that we were just starting that. You know the history prior to that. A lot of fans don't know, but we just started drawing a million fans in 1973, so we didn't hit the 2 million mark until I came out in 1978. Beer Bob says, hey that was great!

We had Bo and Balboni, hitting 22 and 24 homeruns each, but they still didn't prevail and we came in second place in '87—'83 and '87, we were getting there, we were turning it around slowly but surely. We missed out of going to the pennant. You know "Bo Knows" in 87, 22 homeruns, but Bo definitely knows and this Royals team was really starting to see if they could come back to life. We lost out of two games some kind of way and it cost us the first place with the Twins and guess what, the Minnesota Twins won the championship World Series that year against the St. Louis Cardinals, unbelievable, unbelievable. We had a manager change also from Billy Gardner to John Wathan that kind of helped us build our way to the top. In '88, Bo knows. Bo hit 25 homeruns. I mean this guy was awesome. He had 27 stolen bases.

Danny Tartabull was there George Brett, too. George Brett got over the .300 mark again. These guys had come along, but they just could not pull it off. We wound up coming in third place and Tony LaRussa and Oakland came in first place. But it was still a great year for us. We sold a lot of beer; we had a lot of good times. We had many friends from over the years. It was just a fantastic time at Royals Stadium in '88. Watching Bo break his bat over his knees, awesome. Getting riled up with an arm that was like a canon, making catches and hitting balls so far that you could not believe.

But in 1995, a second place finish, 70 wins, 74 losses, the season started late with 1,233,293 fans. That will show you how many fans in Kansas City were turned off because of the strike. It was not just here, but all over the major league basemen and the Beer Men really suffered. We didn't make a lot of money, but we really enjoyed the time we were out there, at least I did, with the fans. I really think about those times we were at home and baseball had not started, sent a shiver up my spine. In 1999, fourth place finish, 64 wins, and 97 losses. 1,506, 088 fans came through the turnstiles. I still sold a lot of beer and met a lot of great folks, a lot of fans.

I can recall back in '99 on June 5th, the weekend series when the Cincinnati Reds were in town and the Royals were looking forward to seeing these teams play. It was such a dismal series with Cincinnati, we wound up loosing that first game on Friday night and didn't follow up on Saturday night, 4-7; and then that Sunday it was just terrible. We got beat 3-14. We didn't have any pitching; it was terrible. We looked forward to the upcoming week.

St. Louis was rolling into town and I remember I had a fan from St. Louis, Rick, and I kept saying, "Monday, Rick, your team is going to lose." The guy came saying, "Beer Bob, we told you we're going to sweep you, this is the first one." Rick had a few beers and we chatted and we had a discussion about how Jorge Orta was called safe at first base. I told him, "Man that was 1985 and this is 1999 and you still hold those thoughts in your head?" That is just how baseball is!

WE BELIEVE!

It really was a sad time for me during 911. Nine eleven 2001 was pretty traumatic for me. The Royals were on the road, and I believe they were going to head to Cleveland next to play. I was at my job, on the 4th floor at City Hall and it really kind of hit home to me. We were going to have a United Way presentation. Buck O'Neal was there and Otis Taylor. I was one of the presenters for the United Way campaign charities called Kansas City Charities. We canceled that because of the terrorist attack on the World Trade Center in

New York. It was a very hard and tough thing for me. When I saw it, tears just started coming down my cheeks. It was sad to think that evil; evil people would take innocent lives in a terrorist attack. Those people were heroes to me in New York. It was a tragedy. We were really fearful for ourselves in City Hall, one of the biggest buildings in downtown Kansas City.

I even lost a church member; she was a guard in the building. She went to my church, Palestine Missionary Baptist Church of Jesus Christ. The whole affair reminded me of the sadness I felt when Dr. Martin Luther King was assassinated in 1968. There were even riots in my neighborhood in 1968 in Kansas City because people felt sad, hopeless and angry. So, I remember it was a real delight to see Coretta Scott King at the ballpark tossing a first pitch in 1985.

Psalms 37:1-3. "Set not thyself between evildoers, neither be thou envious against the workers of iniquity for they shall soon be cut down like the grass and wither as the green earth. Trust in the Lord and do good, so shalt thou dwell in the land and verily though shall be fed." This passage is for all of us that mourned the loss of so many great, great, great citizens of the world and of the United States who lost their lives along with those policemen, firemen, city workers, just regular citizens out trying to help free those folks to get them out of the building to allow them to escape. For all of us, take this to your heart and take this to your thoughts.

When we had our next game at Royals Stadium in September 2001, it really hit home. You could see folks crying in the stands. Beer Bob was crying too. It was a sad time. We are a strong, strong country, and we will continue to survive, because we believe in one another and that is what this country is all about. It was a very difficult time for all of us.

51

In 1998, Tony Muser had moved us to third place with players like Jeff King, Jose Offerman, and Mike Sweeney. There was Carlos Beltran, a 1999 Rookie of the Year, too. Jermaine Dye was a Golden Glover. Mike Sweeney, Joe Randa, and Johnny Damon were ready for the show. But Tony Muser did not know how to talk to the players. Some of the things he said…but Hey joy, what a joy comes in 2002. Guess what, Tony Pena has come through. They got rid of Tony Muser oh so swiftly and sweet. We were happy to see this new Latino Tony speak. He was smooth with the players and as nice as can be. He had a smile on his face for everyone to see. He had his players the way they wanted to play. They loved to play for Tony you say. I know they did because they said, "We love Tony Pena," and I can say, "we love you Tony, just keep up your show because 2003, oh what a show!" Pena was named Manager of the year. Angel Berroa was named Rookie of the Year! Beltran was the Player of the Year and Darrell May was the Royals Pitcher of the Year. But wait; here comes Jose Lima to the mound. It's Lima time! On to 2004!

April 5, 2004,

"41,575 on
Opening Day"

"We're Beer Bob's Customers"

Beer Bob is looking forward to 2005; he is looking forward to selling you a beer if you are twenty-one years of age and more. If you come and see me I will be ready to serve you so true. Don't forget about my buddy Arch, he is always there for you. But Bob is the man and Bob loves one and all. Hey Kansas City fans, let's make this a big call. I know you can bring in 2 million fans or more, let's show them again that Kansas City are the fans. We can do it if you want to, we can make sure that 2 million fans come through the turnstiles that can be true. So please my brothers, my sisters all over, come to the Kauffman Stadium to see our Royals so true. I am still the same Beer Bob on I-70. I may have gotten bigger, I may have gotten wider, but I still sell that beer to all you fans that remember the Royals with pride and laughter.

Come and see us, come on by, we are going to have another World Series time. I know it is coming; it's just a matter of time. Let us all come out and see our Royals change the times. There will be new fans coming through, younger by the dozen. The older fans there that I sold you a beer. There will be younger fans coming when they are 21 and older and buying a beer for the first time from Beer Bob. So come one and come all, come to Kaufman Stadium now. We love to see you now!

It is Bud Light and Beer Bob and I am here to serve you a nice cold Bud Light.

And then there is
Chewy, he sells lemonade.
Lemonade, Lemonade,
Lemonade, Lemonaaaaaade
Wheeeeeeeeeeeew!!!

I sell Bud Light. Yeeeeeeeah, how about an ice cold Bud Light? Come on it is hot, it's hot, it's hot. Beer Bob's got the cold beer here. It's ice cold Bud Light, how about it, how about it? Wanna get one? Looka here, looka here, I check IDs. If you are not 21, you can't buy my wares you see! It's Bud Light, it's Bud Light. Beer Bob says, "always be responsible and have a designated driver."

We have uniforms that are nice and beautiful to see. We have a field that is so gorgeous. We have thousands of awards, it is spectacular all over, and we even have a mini baseball field for children to play. We give our fans appreciation time; we have a Royals Hall of Fame too.

Come on Kansas City! Let's capture the true spirit of our town and build our new stadium now. Look to the west through the downtown loop. Hey folks let's add a monorail to the town to the loop. So fans can come from far and near, so fans look around, look what you see, Kansas City is on the move and the Royals are moving too. We better get back to first place and we better make our city great, because that is the best thing for all of us in Kansas City, we say. We love our Royals. Come to the Stadium right now. Buy a season ticket if you can, if not get the package of twenty games or more or get the small pack, a game at a time, come to the upper deck at any time. Let's fill the Stadium rapidly, let's fill it with gleam, let's make 2 million fans come through, we'll see. Thank you for the memories, thank you Royals fans we so adore. Thank you David Glass for keeping baseball in Kansas City. Thank you Don Glass, Julia Irene Kauffman, Allard Baird, Muzzy Jackson, George Brett, all the Board Directors and all the staff that do so much for our Royals team.

So fans don't forget to buy some peanuts and buy some hotdogs, and buy some Gates Bar-B-Que and buy some pizza, all those things you can get if you like to eat. You can buy a beer from Beer Bob you see. There are plenty of things to do at our lovely stadium you see and don't forget about Sluggerrr; he would love to see you too. He's cruising on his 4-wheeler or dancing on top of the dugout. Sluggerrr likes to throw peanuts, he likes to throw hotdogs. He likes to shoot the hotdogs through the hot dog gun shooter. Catch one if you can!

Bob is here to sell a beer. Beer Bob is here with a cold Bud light, would you like to have one beer tonight? How about a beer, I say to you. Come on and get some of this beer from Beer Bob, he is back. Beer Bob is back, how about a beer? Come on and get another beer from Beer Bob, that's a fact. Hey fans come on out, we will see you soon.

The glare of the sunlight is beaming down as I make my way through the stands to sell one more beer. LAST CALL!!!! It's the bottom of the 8th inning, no more beer sales. I have worked over 2000 games and walked more steps, than I could ever count, but I wouldn't be any place else. I love you Kansas City!

Printed in the United States
By Bookmasters